Diabetes and Our Mob

By Vikki McIntyre
Illustrated by Mila Aydingoz

We respect and honour Aboriginal and Torres Strait Islander Elders past, present and future. We acknowledge the stories, traditions and living cultures of Aboriginal and Torres Strait Islander peoples on this land and commit to building a brighter future together.

Library For All Ltd.

Diabetes and our mob

Have you ever heard your aunties, uncles, or Elders talk about diabetes?

Maybe someone in your family or community has diabetes.

Let's yarn about what diabetes is, why it's important, and what we can all do to keep ourselves and our mob healthy.

What is diabetes?

Diabetes happens when our bodies can't properly use the sugars we get from food. Usually, our bodies turn food into energy with the help of insulin, a special hormone made by our pancreas.

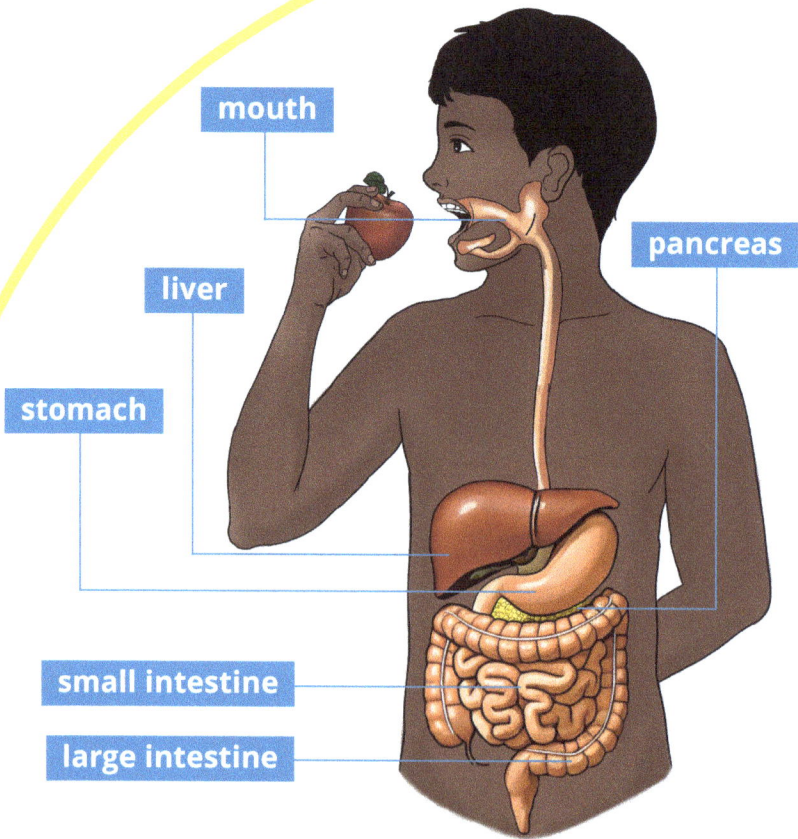

mouth

liver

stomach

pancreas

small intestine

large intestine

But sometimes, the body doesn't make enough insulin or can't use it properly. This means sugar builds up in the blood, causing high-blood-sugar levels, instead of giving us energy.

Food, glucose and the body

- Glucose comes from the food that contains carbohydrate (for example, starch, sugar, rice, pasta, bread, cakes).

- Your mouth, stomach and small intestine digest (break down) food into glucose.

- Glucose enters your blood stream from the small intestine.

- Your blood then carries glucose to your muscles and brain.

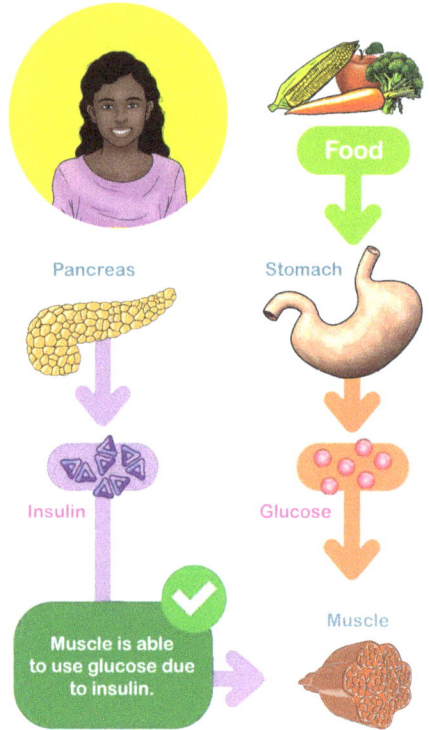

HEALTHY

Pancreas

Food

Stomach

Insulin

Glucose

Muscle is able to use glucose due to insulin.

Muscle

DID YOU KNOW?

There are two main types of diabetes:

- Type 1 diabetes usually starts when we're young, when the body stops making insulin.

- Type 2 diabetes usually happens as we get older, especially if we aren't eating healthy foods or moving our bodies enough.

TYPE 1 DIABETES

Food

Pancreas

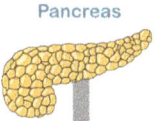

Stomach

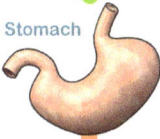

NO insulin

Glucose

Muscle is unable to use glucose due to no insulin.

Muscle

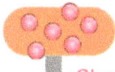

TYPE 2 DIABETES

Food

Pancreas

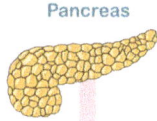

Stomach

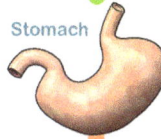

Insulin resistance

Glucose

Muscle is unable to use glucose due to insulin resistance.

Muscle

Why is diabetes common in our communities?

Our mob faces diabetes more than others. There are a few reasons for this.

Diabetes can run in families, which means it is in our genetics.

Many of us have less access to healthy foods and healthcare.

Sometimes it's harder to stay active if we live far from places to exercise or play sports.

Historical factors like colonisation and past policies have impacted the health of our communities. For example, colonisers brought diseases that our bodies find hard to fight.

Stress from racism, inequality, and challenges faced by our communities can also affect health and increase the risk of diabetes.

Knowing and understanding why diabetes happens more in our communities can encourage us to make good choices to stay healthy.

Signs you might have diabetes

It's important to know the signs of diabetes so you can catch it early and get help. These are some common signs.

Feeling very thirsty or hungry, even after eating

Feeling tired a lot, even when resting

Blurry vision, like when things look fuzzy

Cuts or sores taking a long time to heal

Needing to pee more often than usual, especially at night

If you notice these signs, it's important to talk to a trusted adult or see a doctor or nurse straight away.

How can we prevent diabetes?

The good news is we can help prevent diabetes by making some simple changes.

Eat healthy foods:

- Choose fresh fruit and vegetables such as apples, bananas, carrots, and broccoli.

- Swap sugary drinks for water. Water keeps us healthy and strong!

- Try to eat less takeaway food and snacks that are high in sugar and fat.

Stay active:

- Play sport, dance, swim, or go for a walk with family or friends.

- Aim for at least one hour of activity each day.

Stay connected:

- Yarn with Elders, family, and friends to learn more about staying healthy.

- Be together and support each other to make staying healthy easier and more fun.

What should you do if you think you're at risk?

If you're worried that you or someone you know might have diabetes, here's what you can do.

Tell a family member or trusted adult how you're feeling.

Visit your local health clinic or community health centre.

Get a health check-up with your doctor or nurse. They can test your blood-sugar levels easily and quickly.

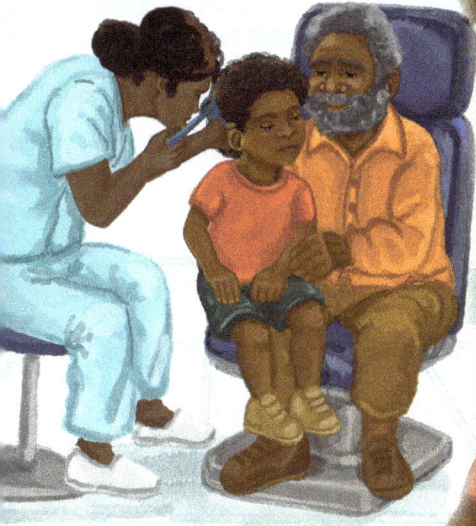

Living strong with diabetes

If someone does have diabetes, it's not the end of the world. With help and care, people with diabetes can still live strong, healthy, and happy lives.

Doctors, nurses, and community health workers can teach you and your family about managing diabetes. This includes eating healthy foods, staying active, and sometimes taking medicine.

Together, we can make sure diabetes doesn't hold us back. Let's support each other, make healthy choices, and keep our mob strong and deadly!

19

Photo Credits

Page	Attribution
Pages 2–3	Amelia Soegijono/austockphoto.com.au
Page 7	courtneyk/istockphoto.com
Pages 12–13	Mukhina1/istockphoto.com
Page 14	Clare Seibel-Barnes/austockphoto.coma.u
Page 15	Thurtell/istockphoto.com

You can use these questions to talk about this book with your family, friends and teachers.

What did you learn from this book?

Describe this book in one word. Funny? Scary? Colourful? Interesting?

How did this book make you feel when you finished reading it?

What was your favourite part of this book?

Download the Library For All Reader app from libraryforall.org

About the author

Vikki McIntyre was born in Sydney and grew up in the western suburbs. Her ancestral Country is the south coast of New South Wales. She descends from the saltwater people of the Dharawal language group. Vikki is happiest when she can feel sand under her feet and smell saltwater in the air.

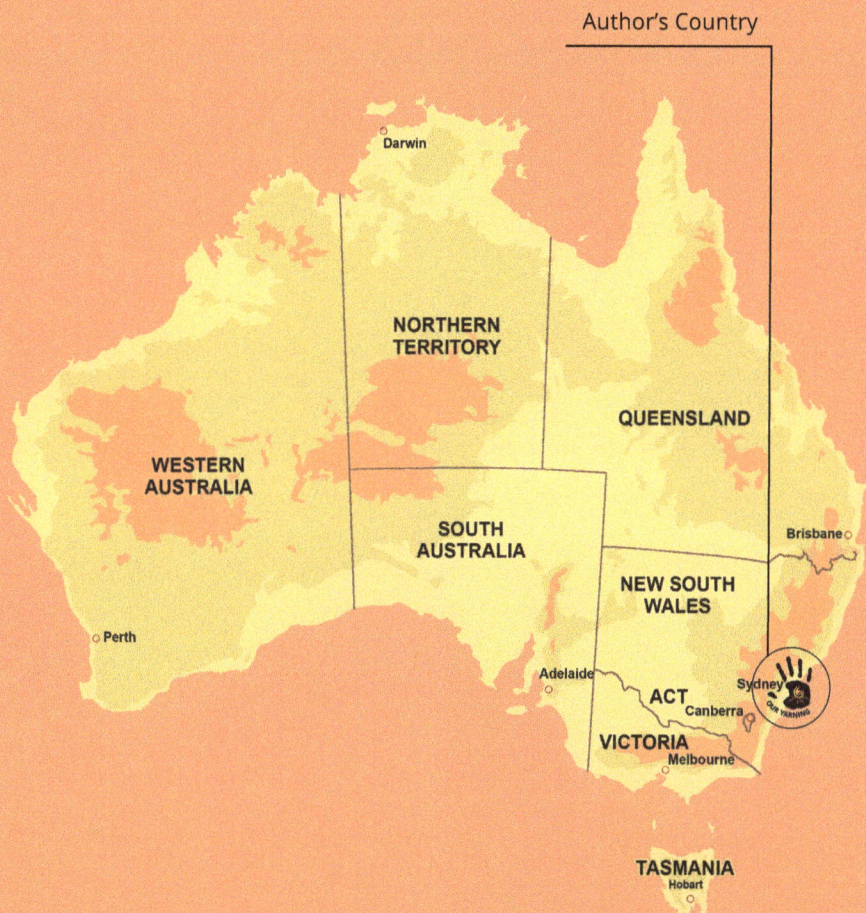

Author's Country

Our Yarning

The Our Yarning collection aligns with the Australian Curriculum through the Cross-Curriculum Priorities — Aboriginal and Torres Strait Islander Histories and Cultures. The collection provides an authentic opportunity for learning and embedding Aboriginal and Torres Strait Islander perspectives because it is written by Aboriginal and Torres Strait Islander people.

We know that children learn better, and enjoy reading more, when they see themselves in the stories, characters and illustrations of the books they read.

To download the app, visit the Google Play Store or Apple Store and search 'Our Yarning'.

You're reading Upper Primary

Learner – Beginner readers
Start your reading journey with short words, big ideas and plenty of pictures.

Level 1 – Rising readers
Raise your reading level with more words, simple sentences and exciting images.

Level 2 – Eager readers
Enjoy your reading time with familiar words, but complex sentences.

Level 3 – Progressing readers
Develop your reading skills with creative stories and some challenging vocabulary.

Level 4 – Fluent readers
Step up your reading skills with playful narratives, new words and fun facts.

Middle Primary – Curious readers
Discover your world through science and stories.

Upper Primary – Adventurous readers
Explore your world through science and stories.

Library For All is an Australian not for profit organisation with a mission to make knowledge accessible to all via an innovative digital library solution. Visit us at libraryforall.org

Diabetes and Our Mob

First published 2025

Published by Library For All Ltd
Email: info@libraryforall.org
URL: libraryforall.org

This book was made possible by the generous contributions of GSK.

Our Yarning logo design by Jason Lee, Bidjipidji Art

Original illustrations by Mila Aydingoz

Diabetes and Our Mob
McIntyre, Vikki
ISBN: 978-1-923554-97-9
SKU04960